Learning How To Help Others

A Guide For Starting & Sustaining An NGO

'Délé A. Sónúbi

DeeSho Books

Person2Person Organization Development and Mentorship

Dedication

This handbook is dedicated to the memory of my friend, the late **Herr Herbert Girkes**, and his wife, Giesela Wahle-Girkes. He was my real-time German teacher who taught me so much about development work and the required critical, analytical, and creative thinking with strong biases for citizen-oriented community development initiatives. These are not possible to learn in any four-walled classroom except on the fields with a good mentor watching.

To the various teachers who allowed me to learn from their strengths and courage and to those who allowed me to mentor them. **The contents of this handbook arose from our interactions, exchanges, and person-to-person l earning.**

Chapters and Topics in This Handbook

Acronyms Used

1. BOT: Board of Trustee

2. CAC: Corporate Affairs Commission

3. CBO: Community Based Organizations

4. COCDI: Citizen-Oriented Community Development Initiatives

5. CSO: Civil society organisation

6. CfP: Call for Proposals

7. ECOWAS: Economic Community of West African States

8. ED: Executive Director

9. EU: European Union

10. FBO: Faith Based Organisation

11. FNF: Fredrich Nauman Foundation (Fredrich Stiftung FNst)

12. GiZ: Deutsche Gesellschaft für Internationale Zusammenarbeit GmbH. Often shortened as GiZ. It is the main German development agency headquartered in Bonn and Eichhorn. It provides services in the field of international development cooperation and international education work.

13. iNGO: International Non Governmental Organization

14. LGA: Local Government Authority

15. LGA: Local Government Areas

16. Logfram: Logical Framework

17. M&E: Monitoring and Evaluation

18. Naira: The name of Nigerian currency

19. NFP: Not for Profit

20. NGO: Non-Governmental Organisation

21. NSA: Non State Actors

22. Okada: Common name used to describe commercial motorcycle riders

23. OVC: Orphan and Vulnerable Children

24. OVI: Objectively Verifiable Indicator

25. P2P: Person To Person

26. ToR: Terms of Reference

27. USAID: United State Aid

About the Mentor

B oth my primary and secondary school education prepared me for the professional path I eventually took. For Tai Solarin, our school proprietor, the essence of life must be measured by personal gains "*We measure life by loss, not by gain; not by the wine drunk but by the wine poured forth!*" I have never wavered in my interest in and commitment to supporting society and the less privileged. My university studies focused on conflict, peace, and social development, and when I returned to Nigeria, I immediately got involved in NGO work and have not looked back for over 22 years. I have worked and collaborated significantly with foreign donor agencies like USAID, the EU, GiZ, the Friedrich Naumann Stiftung (FNF), ECOWAS, and a few regional and Nigerian-based

NGOs. I have therefore acquired sufficient experience to enable me to share my expertise on this topic. I have facilitated several capacity-building projects and mentorships for a sizeable number of NGOs, helping them to expand in their operational and programmatic capacities and also enabling some to acquire their CAC registrations. This number of years I have been around also represents how extensive my exposure is to the standard operation and practise of NGOs, what is required for an NGO to be impactful, and what the rules are for obtaining donor funds. I have made a respectable number of successful grant appraisals and have consulted for some organisations on how to write and win grants. I therefore share part of my lessons learned on this journey.

Acknowledgement

The Agents for Citizen-driven Transformation (ACT) program was designed by the European Union (EU) as its response strategy on the need to invest and engage more with the Civil Society Organisations (CSOs) in Nigeria. This is because the EU has recognised the fact that strengthened Civil Society actors have enormous potential to

contribute to the achievement of sustainable development in Nigeria if their capabilities as 'drivers of change' are enhanced. The ACT programme aims to implement innovative actions that will support the strengthening of institutional mechanisms, structures and processes aimed at improving the internal, external, and programmatic environments of selected CSOs, networks, and coalitions. It also seeks to facilitate an improvement in the current complex regulatory environments, through strategic support that promotes self-regulatory mechanisms amongst selected CSOs, as well as interrogates the possibilities and supports the process of evolving a functional and effective national regulatory framework that will be acceptable to all stakeholders. The ACT programme is funded by the European Union under the 11th European Development Fund and is managed by the British Council. The ACT program is aimed at working with different categories of CSOs selected based on organizational capacity assessment. The program conceives three categories of organizations as follows:

***Emerging CSOs** – operating at the lower community level with minimal recognition and capacity. They do not have organisational systems and processes in place, with very limited financial sources. In some cases, members of the organisation only fund them, and they may not have a business operational space, thus making it very difficult to comply with registration or other legal requirements for its operations.*

***Developing CSOs** –are typically state-based, with some level of recognition in their areas of work but require significant capacity strengthening to improve their internal, programmatic, and relational skills. They have a system of governance in place but may struggle to source the required resources to be fully functional. They have acceptable processes in place for management, financial records, and plans and may have basic or adequate infrastructure to operate and make efforts to ensure ownership at the constituent level. There is limited focus on sustainability as these CSOs may struggle to attract enough financial and human resources to remain fully functional and may lack some skills to manage and operate the CSO, or to fully mitigate against areas of potential risk.*

***Matured CSOs** – well established with significant strength and capacity but require a refresher on areas of their institutional strengthening.*

About The Handbook

This handbook is developed to further support the coaching of the above-described civil society organizations with sound regulatory and support structures. Even though the strong bias of this handbook is for emerging NGOs and also preparing the minds of future volunteers or those who are strongly considering starting an organisation to support people at the community level, this is a handbook that every experienced, non-experienced, and particularly new employee of any civil society organisation should be able to pick up, read, and be sufficiently informed about NGOs, or generally tagged, the development sector, including the histories of CSOs' emergence. This handbook is not only for emerging NGOs; its usefulness cuts across all strata of CSOs.

It is to be noted that the major content of this handbook is borne from the practical experience of the writer and not from theoretical suggestions. Practical examples have been combined with specific recommendations by the government agency responsible for authorizing or registering CSOs.

The strength of this handbook is mentorship on organizational structures, particularly having a functional board of trustees. It was done on purpose; if the organisations engage in proper structure, then they are laying the groundwork for expanding their relevance and staying in business for ages—beyond the founders. And if there are proper leadership structures, then donors and collaborators are happy to support the organizations so they can function and implement their plans to make impacts on their respective communities and target groups. These two are crucial and essential.

It is hoped that this handbook will serve its purposes; it will inform readers and become a basis for developing other targeted handbooks aimed at strengthening promoters and staff of CSOs or ensuring that CSOs can consult it as major reference material as they increase in capacity, impact, and expand their operational competences.

The handbook is divided into three sections.

Section One

This section is used to lay the foundation of civil society organisations. It helps a newcomer to understand the basis of creation or engagements in civil society work (historical perspectives). It also helps in defining some of the roles and functions of CBOs and NGOs. This section helps with conceptual clarifications and lays the groundwork for mentoring already existing organisations.

Section Two

This section is dedicated to mentoring organisations. It starts with mentoring individuals on how to start and maintain an organisation, including the expectations and human resource needs. The mentorship continues with how to build viable organisations, the structures and strategies of CSOs, including CAC registrations, building the organization's leadership contexts, including developing the organogram and raising the BOT, engaging the BOT, and utilising their expertise to build the organisations.

Section Three

Section three deals with the leadership structure of an organisation and how powers are held within civil society organisations. It highlights the position of the BOT, its composition, and its roles. The section also deals with issues of branding, communication, project monitoring and evaluation, etc. The emphasis is placed on the sustainability of the organisation.

The Cry For Help

Undoubtedly, it is possible to make the generalized statement that everyone is endowed with a quality life. But we know this is not usually true. While some have easy access to a decent quality of life, there are some who do not have it as easy as others do. Such is life—the complexity and binary nature of life. In societies where the gaps between the haves and have-nots are so wide, the tendency is to expect a wide range of people who hope for handouts from the rich for as much as they can hang on to. Sometimes, out of moral obligation, the people classified as being privileged voluntarily encourage themselves to assist the less privileged in the best way they know how—which is usually not good enough.

Without being excessively religious or moralistic, helping others is both a gift and a moral obligation. There are those who hardly feel either of these, but for those who have the gift or the moral persuasion to help others, starting a well-structured charity organization offers a good way of doing so. And for this, there are laid-down procedures that are contained in this handbook.

The practicality of assisting others through a structured NGO is that the organization is there to serve the needs of the beneficiaries and provide the required assistance without so much as personalizing the assistance provided to others in a way that makes the beneficiaries worship the philanthropists. The individual behind the organization is free of the burden of the day-to-day struggle to help everyone directly.

Section One: The Evolution of Civil Society Organisations

Collaboration for Social Development

1. Historical Perspectives

Community-based organizations (CBOs) started when some individuals became dissatisfied with the government's response and its inability to resolve social needs and provide supports for the needy. They started by volunteering their time, their money, and their strategic resources to fill in the gap between what the communities needed and what the governments were able to provide. Over time, and through their individual and combined efforts, these "good people" began to organize themselves into recognizable entities and create institutions for helping others.

Today, organizations formed by those individuals have expanded and grown. They have become, among the many names used to describe them, "*development organizations*".

Since these organizations are providing services that governments are constitutionally responsible for providing and are becoming popular and relevant among their target groups and across communities, it became important to identify and mark these development organizations as independent and not government-funded agencies. This is the origin of the expression, intended to describe these organizations as **non-governmental organizations (NGOs),** and their activities are both non-political and particularly those of **not-for-profit organizations**.

Because they are now well identified as non-governmental organizations, different governments at different levels have come up with regulations to moderate the unlimited power of the NGOs. The following are the distinct types of registrations that NGOs must, by law, comply with:

1. A community-based organization must be registered at the level of the local government authority (LGA) where it operates. And the

registration license is limited to these local government areas.

2. A community-based organization that wishes to operate activities beyond its base local government area and cuts into multiple LGAs must be registered at the state level with the state government through designated ministries (i.e., the Ministry of Women's Affairs or the Ministry of Social Affairs).

3. A community-based organization or volunteer organization operating beyond a state in a multiple-state activity must be registered at the federal government (FGN) level. The registration is through the Corporate Affairs Commission (CAC).

With any of these registrations, organizations are free to operate without hindrance from any government operatives or agencies, as long as they comply with the set rules of their respective registrations.

With these regulatory laws, a common identity or umbrella name became **"civil society organizations"**, **"humanitarian organizations"**,

"rights-based organizations," or **"non-state actors"** for NGOs, FBOs, or CBOs, which are all, by characteristic, **not-for-profit organizations.** Another common reference is to nickname members of the CSOs as **"actors,"** so it is common to hear *"civil society actors"* refering to NGO members.

Leadership-by-example is embedded in the policies, strategies, and structures of organizations.

2. Classifications of Organisation

There are different shapes and compositions of organisations operating within the broad development sector. It should be easier to understand each organisation through a generic classification than through its thematic focus or its sectoral composition. Many of these organisations have multiple thematic foci with wide-ranging target issues. The following are different classes into which organizations are boxed:

2.1. Civil Society Organizations (CSOs):

CSO is an umbrella name used to describe or classify all not-for-profit and non-governmental organizations.

The thematic representation for CSO is broad, and it is focused on bringing changes to society. Civil Society Organisations, in a broader sense also include organisations that are not particularly targeting society development but are associations of self-interest groups. Civil society organizations play very vital roles in helping to shape societies, forge development-oriented growth, pursuant of rights, defense of abuses, and promotion of community cohesion, among many others.

Member organizations that form CSOs

1. *NSA—Non-State Actors (Another name for CSOs coined by the EU)*

2. *NGO: Non-Governmental Organization*

3. *CBO: Community- Based Organization*

4. *FBO—Faith- Based Organizations*

5. *INGO: International Non-Governmental Organization*

6. *Associations (i.e., Market Women's Association, Laborers' Union, Trade Union, etc.)*

7. *Cooperatives*

8. *Networks*

9. *Platforms*

2.2. Community-Based Organizations (CBOs):

These are organizations that work to empower people, build cohesion, and bring positive changes and development to people at the community level. They are practically based in the communities where they work. Wikipedia describes CBOs as "*organizations aimed at bringing desired improvements to a community's social health, well-being, and overall functioning.*" Examples of CBOs include trade associations such as

1. *Market women's association*

2. *Landlord Association*

3. *Auto Mechanic Associations*

4. *Okada Riders' association*

5. *Koloba and Lala Progressive Women's Associations*

6. *Ìkénné Residents Union, etc.*

2.3. Non-Governmental Organization (NGO):

It is an umbrella name used to describe organizations that provide social services, help, and support to communities and societies, which are performing responsibilities that are naturally government responsibilities, but they are described as non-governmental organizations" to mark them as different from government, its institutions, or agencies.

1. *Rotary Club and Lions' Club*

2. *Society for Family Health*

3. *Africa Leadership Forum*

4. *The African Foundation for Environment and Health*

2.4. Faith-Based Organizations (FBOs):

Faith-based organizations are organizations that represent faith institutions such as churches, mosques, orthodox faith institutions, traditional religious institutions, and so on. Faith-based organizations serve as religious instrumentalities of social transformation in contemporary times. Traditionally, faith-based organizations have directed their efforts toward meeting the spiritual, social, and cultural needs of their members, but in modern terms, they have expanded their relevance to include others who do not share their faith. Examples are the following:

1. *Christian Association of Nigeria (CAN)*

2. *Federation of Muslim Women Association of Nigeria (FOMWAN)*

3. *Christian Aids*

4. *Catholic Women's Association*

5. *The Young Men and Women Christian Association*

(YMCA)

6. *The Christian Health Association of Nigeria (CHAN)*

7. *Christian Rural and Urban Development Association of Nigeria (CRUDAN)*

8. *Justice, Development, and Peace Commission (JDPC)*

2.5. Non-State Actors (NSAs):

The European Union, under its ACP Country partnership policies called the Cotonou Agreement (June 2000)[12] was one of the first to use this broad classification and all-inclusive definition of development organizations in Nigeria by widening the definition net under an all-inclusive umbrella name. This is a broad name given to organizations to shelter every organization that is ordinarily uncategorized but shares similar characteristics with NGO and not-for-profit organizations. Previously excluded organizations such as philanthropic foundations (*i.e.*, rotary club), academic institutions (academic staff union), and business associations (i.e., barbers association, *Okada* union, property owner association, etc.) are now included in the classification of development organizations and extended the same benefits such as tax incentives as they give NGOs but now called NSAs. But with the new umbrella name, NSA allows all organizations and individual activities that are not personal or family-owned to be classified as development organizations and receive support from local or international donors.

For the purpose of this handbook, we will use the intermediary umbrella name Civil Society Organization" (CSO) to refer to organizations doing activities that are not for profit, non-maximization of profit, non-governmental, and voluntary.

3. Relevance and Functions of CSOs

A friend once asked me to help him understand the relevance of NGOs and the work we do. I asked him to close his eyes and imagine a world without these men and women who risk their lives and health to ensure that rights are protected and semblances of justice are accorded to the oppressed and denied; to imagine a community without that philanthropist who thinks he must give back to the society that gave birth to him and be charitable to her people first before spreading her wealth to others; to make lives more tolerable for the elderly, the weak, the orphans, and the vulnerable; to imagine there are no experts who readily jump into disaster areas and prevent catastrophes such as Ebola, malaria, cholera, and courageously aim at the global eradication of polio and so on. And if you can imagine a world without the contributions of these men and women as volunteer social services advocates, interfaces, and providers, then the relevance or otherwise of NGOs is easily explained. Anyone still curious about the relevance of civil society groups only needs to visit countries at war, nations in conflicts, natural disasters, or states ravaged by epidemics, and they will appreciate the tremendous work CSOs do and the huge resources they put into making lives easier for the people and liveable for all (the target population). The enormous risks to personal lives, injuries, and emotions that CSO actors face to stand in the gap between the people (the wounded, the deprived, the homeless, the maimed, and the sick, etc.) and the government by promoting healing and reconciliation, providing food and medical aids, creating awareness and confidence in the use of vaccines, getting rid of hazardous content that can create epidemics, etc. The fight against HIV/AIDS, the struggle to vaccinate communities against diseases, the recent global epidemic of COVID-19, the efforts to help those who cannot help themselves and the activities of CSOs to feed the poor and the needy during lockdowns are further testaments and pointers to the relevance of CSOs.

3.1. Relevance:

The impact and relevance of CSOs or CBOs in the lives of people at community levels cannot be overemphasized. The emergence of CSOs or CBOs in the first place was because of the government's inability to satisfy the needs of its citizens. Governments may not have "eyes" or a presence everywhere, but CBOs, by their nature and function, know their communities very deeply; they know the community residents, the visitors, the estimated number of residents, and the issues concerning the communities, the core and true natures of the needs. CBOs have listening ears to the problems of society without thinking of getting votes to win elections in return. They are genuinely concerned and can be more effective than governments and their agencies.

3.2. Functions of Civil Society:

The generic functions of the CSO, irrespective of its thematic focus, are the following:

1. **Expressing and representing the needs of the communities**: One of the core competencies of these organizations is becoming voices for the voiceless and a beacon of hope for the oppressed. CBOs, FBOs, and NGOs are very close to their target groups and the people they represent. Most of the time, they live within the target communities, which makes it easier to feel the pulse of the people, and as a result, they are able to effectively advocate for the target groups.

2. **Community Building: Community building is part of the functions of the CBOs**: They build communities where peace, development, growth, and prosperity will be the landmarks of their achievements. Part of the purpose of setting up a CBO is to build community and strengthen its members better than they were before the

engagement of the CBOs. The community building function also includes:

3. **Community cohesion building**: It is part of the responsibility of CSOs to seek cohesion amongst residents of communities or countries, to mediate conflicts, to improve understanding of government policies, and to help build trust and strengths where such are lacking. Examples are through reconciliatory missions, conflict resolution mechanisms, and community dialogues.

4. **Facilitating the human, social, and political entitlements**: The relevance and legal standing of CSOs is to collaborate with relevant institutions in building a stable and credible political system. CSOs work for political stability and justice. A politically stable country is a result of the competence and proper functioning of the CSOs.

5. **Facilitating Social and Economic Development: Social and economic development** is a real impact area for CBOs and CSOs. This refers

to building the well-being and the economic upliftment of the people living in the target areas. No NGO will lay claim to the continued impoverishment of its target groups if there are ways of eradicating their poverty. CSOs help in the areas of

1. Poverty alleviation

2. Microfinance facilities

3. Grant and sub-grant facilities

4. Skills and vocational training enhancements

5. Cooperatives

6. Women's loan schemes

7. Farmers' loan schemes, etc. and

8. Orphans and Vulnerable Children Support Funds

6. **Partaking in government policy promotion and implementations**: CSOs are encouraged and most often invited by the government to share responsibilities in popularizing government policies and facilities, such as

1. Voters' registration campaign

2. Voters' awareness campaign

3. *Vaccinations*

4. *Polio eradication campaign*

5. *Population census*

6. *Children's immunizations*

7. *Breastfeeding campaign*

8. *National Orientation, etc.*

CSOs are also encouraged to operate within the context of the government's policy provisions. For the implementation of some specific government policies, governments have always relied on the support of CSOs, particularly CBOs, to collaborate and popularize such policies and developments. For example, governments have had to rely heavily on CSOs to broaden the spread of electoral laws through election awareness activities conducted by the CSOs. There are not many government outreaches that are as broad as the outreach of the CSOs. CBOs are relied on to help in the popularization (often referred to as mobilization) and promotion of vaccines, breastfeeding, birth control, and awareness on the spread of diseases such as polio, HIV, COVID-19, and so many others.

A personal Motivation:

Bi mo l'owo, ma fi yin Oluwa Olupese;
Oba to da mi Bi mo l'owo, ma fi yin O o,
Olugbala; Dun mi dun mi ninu ye o Baba
Yungba yungba, k;aye ko yemi
Yungba yungba, k'aye dara fun mi
Yungba, yungba, k'aye yemi, kin ma m'osi
Dunmi dnumi ninu ye o e Baba

Section Two: Coaching and Mentoring CSOs

Mentoring JDPMC
Oshogbo, 2011

4. Starting A Social Development Organization

Starting a development organization requires good knowledge of its foundation. There are four suggested basic principles that must be adhered to when starting a CSO. They are the intentions, the passion, the dedication or commitment, and the structures. Starting a development organization (CSO) requires the following:

4.1. The Intention:

A desire to start a development organization, otherwise known as an NGO, starts first with the "why." What are the intentions behind wanting to engage with such an organization? The clarity of the intention helps shape how the organization will operate (what it will engage in and what it will not engage in). In this case, the intention is to do common good. The goal and reason for creating the organization must be clear to both the founder and partners who are invited to either join or collaborate with the project.

4.2. The Passion:

This has to do with the emotions behind the intention; the founder's inner man must identify that something is wrong in the community, and s/he wants to correct the wrong. Passion is the drive and commitment to want to keep society together and to want to support people who need it most.

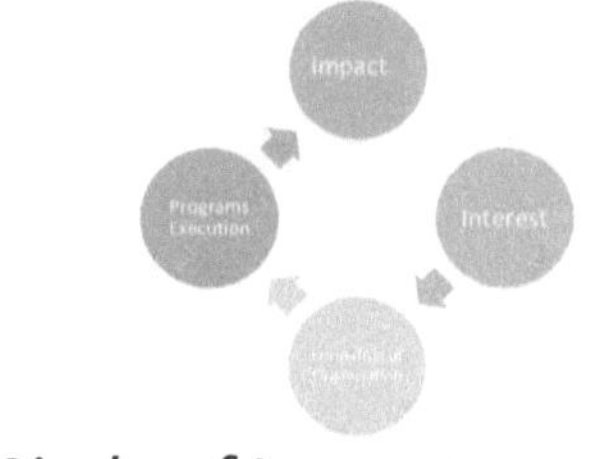

Circle of Impact

4.3. The Dedication:

Dedication to an organization and its activities requires time and resources that are to be spent on creating and sustaining such support-based organizations. Time is what is spent, forsaking other occupations to be available for the NGO project. Resources are both human and material (including financial) resources needed to keep the organization and its various projects and programs going.

4.4. The Structure:

Structure is the mechanism that keeps all the visions, missions, and other goals of the organization in their required forms. What is worth doing at all is worth doing well. Structure is required to build the organization in such a way that it runs like a system that ensures the easy flow of activities and the management of human and material resources. Structure refers to what to know, what to do, how to do it, and the best way to do it.

Chapter Five

5. Organizational Strategy and Policy

5.1. Organization Strategy:

The goal of every development organization and CSO is not only to be relevant with a large membership but also to expand, increase activities, and record impacts in the lives of the target groups. This is the essence of CSOs and the reason politicians fear them most: because they make recognizable impacts. To make an impact and increase impact, the key operational success factor is the strategy of the organization. Organizational strategy (OS) refers to the set of activities and actions an organization embarks on in order to create the impact it seeks. In another word, organization strategy is the strategic tool for an organization's effectiveness and long-term standing. Without an organizational strategy, organizations will perform their intervention work on the basis of impulses and "good" feelings. No organization is sustained on impulses and good feelings; organizations last long beyond their foundation members when there are organizational structures and strategies for remaining impactful and relevant. The sum total of activities and tools collectively deployed by the organization for impact and sustainability form the organization's strategy.

As the above diagram indicates, having good intention to support the community is not enough, there are other things to add together before impacts are made.

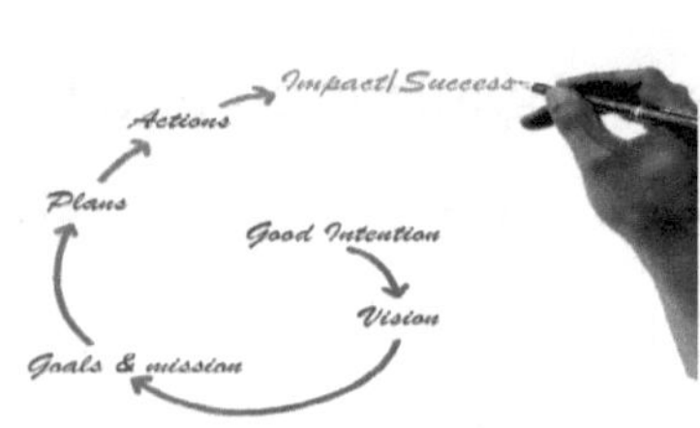

Circle of Impact

5.2 Organizational Structure:

An organizational structure is a system that outlines how certain activities are directed in order to achieve the goals of an organization. These activities can include

1. Rules guiding the modus operandi of the organization

2. Roles of staff and volunteers and other actors in the organization, and

3. Responsibilities for actions taken or not taken.

The organizational structure also determines how information flows between levels of personnel within the organization. Organizational structure points at how the organization manages its style of work, its internal matters (including managing its internal crisis), reaching its goals, fulfilling its roles and obligations (legal and social obligations), and how it projects its image and expands its base.

To be well structured, the organization requires, at the very beginning, to set up and clarify its aims and objectives.

5.3. Aim and Objectives:

Setting up an organization of this nature requires a reason(s). It is not logical to wake up one morning and say, "Now this organization is formed. If this is the case, then it is not a serious thing that will endure the test of time. A serious intention must have an aim. The following questions are pertinent:

1. What is the aim of setting up this organization or enterprise? (*For example, the aim of this organization is to improve the lives and wellbeing of the residents of Ayobo.*)

2. What does the organization intend to achieve with such an enterprise? (*For example, to create a peaceful co-existence amongst the people of Koloba and Lala community*)

3. What is the justification for such an enterprise? (*For example, due to the declining standards of living and bad economic situations in the local government area, our economic empowerment will enable people to engage in self-generated incomes.*)

4. Is this the best time to set up such an enterprise? (*For example, due to the COVID-19 lockdown in the state, most residents have lost their means to*

generate income. (They need the help to recover from their abject poverty.)

5. What are the necessary inputs for setting up this enterprise? (*For example: a functional office where people can visit, with qualified staff, volunteers, and skilled and willing donor partners.*)

If these questions are not asked at the time of setting up the organization, they can still be raised at a later point so that it becomes easier to set up the structure of the organization. Aims are the expression of the overall intention—what you hope to achieve by creating the organization.

5.4. Objectives:

Objectives are the steps taken to achieve the organization's aim. This is where you make the project tangible by saying how you are going to go about it. There is no law that says the objectives for setting up an organization must be ones.

What is necessary to note is that objectives have to be

1. practicable

2. realistic,

3. achievable, and

4. doable (with consideration of available resources).

There is no point in having objectives that are gigantic and incredulous or something in the air. Objectives must be down to earth, humble, and create room for greater achievements, i.e., that the organization can achieve more than its set objectives during operation.

Examples of objectives for organizations of this nature are as follows:

1. to create opportunities for people in rural communities to access means of livelihood with preferences for women, girls, and youths

2. to improve the socio-economic status of people in rural communities, especially women, girls, and youths, through microcredit facilities, skills acquisition programs, and vocational training.

3. to improve the educational standard of people in rural communities, with a special focus on girl

child education.

4. to improve the health conditions of people in rural communities through medical services and outreach programs.

5. to render humanitarian support to rural communities through the provision of portable water

6. to improve the living standards of vulnerable groups through the provision of food and other relief items.

7. to eliminate violence against women and girls in rural communities through dialogue, advocacy, awareness creation, sensitization, and collaboration with other like-minded organizations.

A significant thing to note about objectives is that they are specific, they are measurable, and they have a defined completion date.

5.5. Goals:

Goals are the perceived outcomes of your interventions. Goals are the general guidelines that explain what you want to achieve in your community and amongst your target groups. Goals must be reasonable and must be an easy aim. For example, if you intend to pay school fees for girls' education or to pay for the examination of some pupils, what is the goal there? The goal is not the fees; the goal is to see a girl child educated; the goal is an educated girl child (which is the outcome of paying school fees or paying for examination); that is what is hoped for, the object of achievement.

5.6. Strategies, Policies and Procedure:

Here is where the organization's strategies are clearly stipulated. This clarity contains how the organization will be run, the manner of implementation of program activities, the recruitment procedures, the staff handbook, the organization's policies (which could change as the season progresses and needs arise), and other formalities for handling internal dynamics, conflict resolution, and public presentations of the organization. The organization's strategic document includes such elements as:

5.7. Vision Statement:

This is a statement that explains the project as conceived by the individuals who started the organization. A "vision statement is a statement of what the organization wishes to become. It is an expression of a dream for the future of the community and the organization. A vision statement is a description of where you're going. Vision must be very broad and must not be of a project that will finish in an immediate future. A vision gives leverage to the continued running of the organization. A vision is futuristic. A vision must be open-ended. A vision statement describes the organization's purpose, what it is striving for, and what it wants to achieve. Writing a vision statement gives the organization an opportunity to better articulate the characteristics that influence the organization's strategy.

Vision Statement: A future where people living in rural communities especially women and girls enjoy life of dignity, freedom from societal limitations and are empowered to reach their full potentials

5.7.1. Characteristics of a Vision Statement:

1. **A vision must be an open-ended statement of what the founders see ahead** (this means a statement that does not suggest a limitation of scope or areas of activity).

2. **A vision is about what the founders want to achieve** through the organization—what exactly is the goal; what will the organization be aiming for? What is (are) the aim(s) of setting up the platform (CSO)?

3. **A vision statement is not "period-specific" or "period-bound,"** meaning it cannot say it will end by a future date. It must be a wish that cannot be achieved in a specific lifetime. (i.e., a vision to see every girl child educated is a statement of never-ending activities because there will always be a new girl child after one is already trained.)

4. **A vision of an organization is allowed to be capture of a gigantic dream and not suggestive of little achievements** (for example, a vision for economically empowered women is so gigantic because women's population is not small, and if economic empowerment is a vision to make women millionaires, how small is this dream?)

An example of a vision statement borrowed from an organization is as follows:

A future where people living in rural communities, especially women and girls, enjoy a life of dignity, freedom from societal limitations, and are empowered to reach their full potential.

5.8. Mission Statements:

A mission is a statement of how you will accomplish your vision. "Vision" is where the organization is going; "Mission" is how to get there. The strength of an organization's mission is dependent on its comprehensive understanding and well-articulated vision. To further understand a mission statement, what would be the processes through which the vision is achieved or pursued?

5.9. Registration:

It is a legal requirement for CSOs to be registered, irrespective of the biases that are behind the clamor for registration. In Nigeria, the government has provided for such registration for the purposes of accountability and statistics. The government has provided for different levels of registration depending on the purpose and coverage of the CSO. The different levels of registration are:

- Local Government Authority (LGA) level (naturally, this will be where the organization is cited and not any other by proxy). In case the organization intends to work in multiple LGAs, then each LGA registration will be separately submitted.

- (Respective) State Government level, which

is more prudent than seeking different LGA registration each time the project wants to expand. This is also strategic in case the intention of the organization, right from the beginning, is to expand from one to engage in multiple LGA levels, and

- Federal government level, e.g., registration with the Nigeria Corporate Affairs Commission.

The Corporate Affairs Commission's registration requirements are:

1. Application to the Registrar General with XYZ Naira as application fees and two proposed names of the organization.

2. The names and phone numbers of each of the proposed trustees and the secretary are also provided.

3. Valid ID card of each proposed trustee and the secretary. It must be a government-issued ID card, e.g., an international passport, a driver's license, or a national ID card. Email addresses, dates of birth,

and home addresses of the proposed trustees.

4. Aims and objectives of the organization.

5. Proposed constitution, which must include the minimum number of trustees, the maximum number of trustees, and the tenure of trustees.

6. There will be a newspaper publication announcing the name of the organization. The proposed organization must make a financial commitment for the newspaper publication costs, depending on the newspapers used.

7. The trustees' declarations will cost XYZ Naira each, depending on the number of trustees.

8. The incorporation of the trustee's fee will cost XYZ. Naira.

9. Minutes of the meeting where trustees were appointed.

10. The professional fee is for the lawyer who helps prepare the application. This will depend on

whether a lawyer is engaged for the purpose of the registration processes, including filing at CAC. This can also be done by any knowledgeable and experienced consultant.

11. Pay the filing fee.[1]

5.10. Organogram:

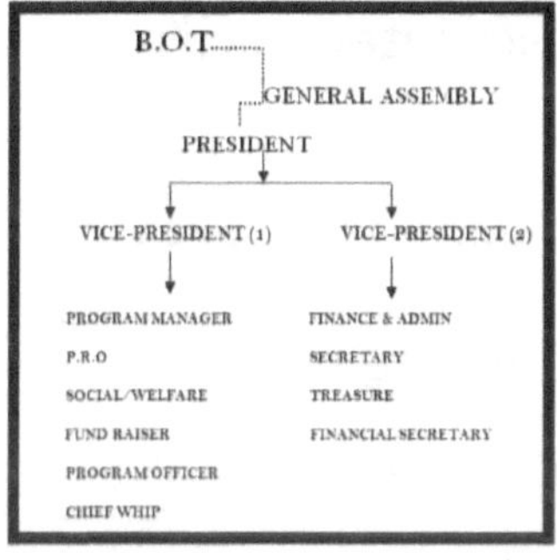

Sample organogram of Membership based org.

The organogram is a physical and graphical representation of staff positions, leadership styles, and chains of responsibility within the organization. It is physical because most donors expect organizations to display it on their notice boards in the office for visitors, friends, and partners to see the moment they enter their offices. It is graphical because it is not written in words but described in designs with arrows going either downward or upward, indicating points of leadership, reporting patterns, and responsibility policies.

Organograms are one of the best and most instant ways of explaining the relationships between staff, leaders, where final authority lies, and other structures within an organization.

> **Note 1**: Some donors or foreign partners are reluctant to commit their funds to an organization when they are not clear about the leadership structure of that organization. The reluctance is often associated with an unexplained or unclear demarcation of authority between the executive director and the finance team. Part of the reason donors insist on a proper organogram is that, where there are no clear templates for transparency and accountability (which an organogram ensures), grants handled within the organization are likely to be mismanaged, misappropriated, or grossly unaccounted for.

With the organogram, a donor sitting in Australia, for example, knows there is a board of trustees that oversees the executive director and the excesses of that person and that the finance manager cannot resolve to misappropriate resources. The organogram explains the system of checks and balances the organization deplores in its operation and management of resources.

One of the mentorship techniques that emerging organizations must adhere to is being mentored to have a comprehensive and well-designed organogram. This is essential for two reasons:

1. One needs to organize the leadership pattern of the organization for staff to know where they are in the scheme of things and how they are placed in the sequences of accountability and transparency, as well as how staff promotion will rise along the ladders.

2. Aside from donor expectations, the Nigerian registration authority, the CAC, insists that for organizations to be registered, they must have and present an organogram. This means the function of an organogram in an organization is not a mere role but something of strategic importance and essential to the organization's appraisal.

Note 2: Having a full and comprehensive organogram with all the functions in it does not mean that every position on the organogram is already filled by staff. It also does not mean that the organogram will be restricted to the existing staff only. With a full organogram, the organization is telling itself that there will be vacancies to fill the gaps in the future.

5.11. Employee/Staff Handbook:

An employee handbook is often similarly called a staff handbook, an employee manual, or a company policy manual. All the names refer to the same thing. The staff handbook contains information related to the organization's history, mission, values, policies, procedures, and benefits in a written format. This is very valuable communication material for an employee, given by the employer upon the employee's invitation to start work.

This employee handbook is used to explain the work policies, work ethics, the work environment, and the work cultures to new recruits. It is used to bring together employment-related issues and job-related information that employees need to know.

Some related functions of the staff/employees handbook that CSOs must note are that the employee handbook:

1. Explains common practices that are currently in place.

2. Employee handbook gives general information, particularly about holiday arrangements, the organization's marriage and child-bearing policies, non-statutory policies (i.e., policies not required by law), and so on.

3. The handbook also gives case-specific information on organization policies, rules, disciplinary policies, conflict management, grievance-solving procedures, and other information modelled after national labor laws and edicts.

Note 3: Staff handbooks are not restricted to corporate organizations alone. It is a document used in general organizational contexts. If there are no policies in place, the CSO should develop one as a matter of practicality so as to create a culture document that everyone must adhere to and that the organization can also use to shield itself from accusations of discrimination, unfair treatment, and claims of rights abuse.

Organogram

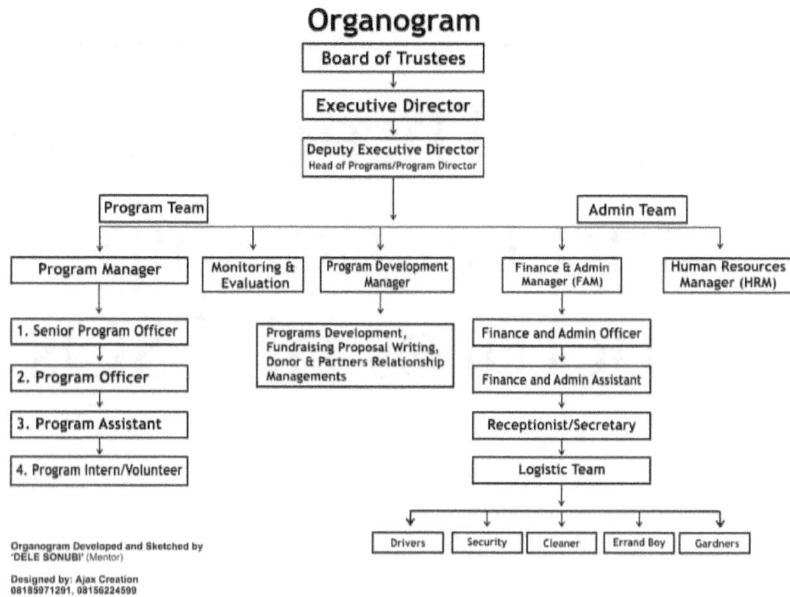

A standard, comprehensive flow of functions for an already well-established organisation. Organisations are encouraged to have this kind of flow with distinct office and relationship flow, both up and down. It is also not unusual to have multiple program officers, each handling different portfolio or sectorally-allocated roles.

Section Three: Power and Leadership Structures of CSOs

6. Power and Leadership Structures of CSOs

A leadership strata in an organisation gives a picture of the levels of responsibilities pertaining to the broad overview of everything in the organisation. It contains both a strategic and an operational overview. Strategic is the intellectual part—the thinking, the decision-taking, the harnessing of different energies in the organisation. While operation is the actual work, the physical function roles in the organisation. The topmost leadership role oversees everyone and their functions in the organisation and provides the deep-thinking decisions to be taken and implemented. As staff grows in the hierarchy of the orgonogram, such staff begins to come closer to combining and sharing responsibilities in both overview roles of "strategic" and operations." This leadership strata is visually contained in the organisation's adopted organogram but whatever the style of organogram the organisation adopts, its leadership is essentially headed by the Boar of Trustees (BoT).

It is commonly agreed that CSOs are very powerful given the level of social control they have over their target populations. In particular, it is hard to defeat a vibrant CSO in popularity contest within a target base. They have the tricks; they understand the strategies; they speak the paralinguistic languages; and they feel the pulse of the target groups. CSOs also have the people's trust—more than government actors can get. CSOs are so powerful because they achieve concrete and measurable impacts in the lives of their beneficiaries. Although these actors in civil society do not seek elections or votes, they command significant respect and patronage among the people.

Note 1: Civil society is a key agent of change. Civil society organizations amplify the voices of people, defending their human rights and demanding that their concerns be addressed. Civil society also holds governments, public institutions, and the private sector to account for their commitments.[4]

Similarly, donor organizations invest so much resources—as grants or other forms of support—in CSOs, hoping that the volunteered resources will be used for their intended purpose, helping to cushion the effects of the identified social challenges. As a result, CSOs are sometimes in control of resources that are often practically not legally accountable to the public but only to the donors that gave the grants.

For this reason, there is a need to monitor and control the power structures of CSOs and to impose recognisable leadership models on them so that it is easier to monitor their excesses with appropriate checks in place to avoid abuse of office and resources.

An organogram displays the Board of Trustees (BOT) as the head of that organization, followed by the Executive Director and his or her team. In this way, power within the organization is diffused and decentralized among all layers, with checks and balances in appropriate places.

> *This power diffusion makes it possible, for example, for a finance secretary to say no to the ED when he or she makes an illicit demand for money and not suffer any repercussions because a rift emanating from this illegitimate demand will be taken to the board level for final resolution.*

The BOT is conceived as the check-and-balance structure of an organization. It enjoys the highest level of political and administrative power in the organization. This means every other staff member and/or consultant indirectly reports to the board through the identified channels of reporting. CAC recognizes the board with absolute power. CAC also provides a minimum required number of two members of the board, while the maximum can be at the organization's discretion because there is no legal maximum but should be within a reasonable limit.

> ***Note 2:*** *Reasonably, it is prudent for an organization to have between four and five board members for reasons of logistics and modest management of the board. Convening a board meeting is a very expensive task. Fitting logistic arrangements for a board meeting, such as hotel reservations, payment for the venue of the meeting, transport reimbursement, feeding arrangements, and per diem, all require a lot of money and time to put together. So, wisdom encourages an organization to adopt the minimum rather than exploring a large number of BOT members.*

The CAC's mandate provides the organization with a window to convene Board meetings at least twice a year. While there is no statutory maximum, the total number of board meetings must be written in the organization's constitution. If the organization has not been doing this before, it therefore stands at variance with the law and requirements of the CAC. This means the leadership of the organization could be in legal trouble if CAC chooses to look into their activities. Oversight functions of NGOs are within the purview of CAC, and organizations might be in a mess of legal exposure if they have not complied with laid-down regulations. "The doctrine of *clean hands is based on the maxim of equity, which states that one who comes into equity must come with clean hands. This doctrine requires the court to deny equitable relief to a party who has violated good faith with respect to the subject of the claim*." Where organizations have not fulfilled these requirements (convening board meetings), the solution is to do the right thing immediately rather than wallowing in potential legal jeopardy. It is never too late to activate the Board and convene them for a proper briefing about the developments and activities of the organisation and the extent to which the organisation's visions are being achieved. Every Board meeting must have comprehensive minutes of the meeting professionally captured and effectively documented. It is good during legal procedure and documents that CAC might be interested in whenever oversight functions are being carried out.

6.1. The Board of Trustee:

Whatever number of trustees the organization chooses, whether a four- or five-member board, the composition of the board has a certain characteristic:

1. The individual to be selected as a board member need not be a wealthy man or woman. Wealth as a criterion is not an encouraging reason to pick a member to add to the organization's board. This is because a rich board member is usually not practically willing to commit to attending meetings or sit through long discussions and or commit his personal money to run the organization. Often times, rich people are more miserly than people perceive them to be. Also, for all intents and purposes, some rich men or women do not necessarily have time for not-for-profit activities but are majorly occupied with activities that bring them maximum profits. However, there are few outstanding rich men and women with

hearts of giving and the attitude of helping, combined with a love for humanity, and this small group can be a practical addition to the board.

2. The individual doesn't have to be a socialite of high esteem, the chief of a community, the most influential person in a community, a captain of industry, or someone best known to everyone. A Yoruba proverb has it that "*Káa tó fi ènìyàn joyè láarín ìlú óní láti jé eni rere*" (community honors are reserved only for the morally upright or someone best known to everyone). A Yoruba proverb has it that "Kaa to fi eniyan joye laarin ilu on lati je enirere" (community honors are reserved only for the morally upright). The same idea in Igbo is "Ezi agha ka ego". The simple availability of an individual to be added as a board member or the simple indication of an individual's willingness to volunteer his or her time and resources as a board member are more than sufficient and honorable. The reason for this is that a social elite, a chief, a popular jingo, the most famous man or woman in the community, may not have time to:

A Attend the scheduled board meetings.

B Offer his guidance and leadership for the organization.

C Be available for consultation whenever the organization requires that.

However, a simple and uncomplicated board member has not only the time but also the wisdom to share when called upon.

3. The proposed board member does not have to be an intellectual, a guru, or a well-known person; he or she can be someone with a special gift for people, someone with native intelligence, or someone rich in "common sense." These are some of the values that the organization need to move forward and make impacts.

6.2. Functions, Roles and Responsibilities of BOT:

The existence of BOT is statutory, but the roles and responsibilities of BOT are both statutory and evolving. Some of the roles and responsibilities are

1. **Provide leadership**: It is expected that the board will play the statutory role of providing the ultimate leadership and guidance in the organization; the final power and authority rest with the board. As a consequence, the board members have the statutory power to remove the founder from the organization or redirect the structure of the organization beyond the imagination of its founder. The board has such power and more. This is why it is extremely important for an organization's founders and owners to be well guided and reasonable while choosing board members.

2. **Assist in fund raising**: This particular role or responsibility is hardly explored by organizations, but it is important because one of the reasons for inviting an individual to join the board is so as to use his experience during resource mobilization. And one of such ways is to leverage their vast networks as strategic supports for the organization when required. So, board members are expected to join the leader of the organization when trying

to raise capital or embarking on large projects. It is also common for individual members of the BOT to make donations to the organization and bail it out during times of financial challenges.

3. (*Senior*) **Staff recruitment:** It is expected that the final recruitment for an Executive Director of the organization will be done by the BOT. Senior or principal officers cannot be recruited without the knowledge of the BOT. The BOT sets and determines performance standards and evaluates the performance of the ED on an annual basis.

4. **Policy guidance**: Every major or minor policy decision of the organization, every policy review, every policy change, and every policy introduction must get the approval of the board before they are made final or operational. The BOT is also to determine whether the CSO should continue as an organization or whether it has outlived its usefulness.

5. **Finance and fiscal accountability**: The Board, through its selected committee on finance and

fiscal responsibility, has the statutory powers to:

1. Review and approve the organization's annual budgets.

2. On an annual basis, to review and approve a spending policy (*determining the amount of money that will be available for its target sectors)* for the organization and an investment policy that fulfills the mission and goals of the organization.

3. Through its directly relevant committee or sub-committee, the BOT has the statutory responsibility of providing financial and fiscal oversight for the Finance and Administration department of the organization.

4. On an informal level (meaning this is a solidarity obligation and not a statutory one), the BOT is also encouraged to help bail out the organization during periods of financial crises by considering some donations or facilitating practical facilities that help navigate through the turbulent period.

5.

Oversee the work of the Finance Committee in defining investment goals, monitoring the management of investments, and to tax requirements and all other statutory and non-statutory obligations.

6. **To establish and oversee strategic policy**: Some policy decisions and strategic policy positions of the organization fall under the statutory roles of the BOT. The BOT must approve and oversee:

a. Institutional policies which includes, but are not limited to, a policy of non-discrimination.

b. Ensuring gender balance in both programs and recruitments of the organization

c. Personnel policy development and implementation

d. Mechanisms for fiscal accountability

e. To take responsibility for planning by

f. Ensuring that there is a mission statement.

g. Ensuring that there is a vision statement.

h. Ensuring that there are strategic policies and a strategic plan in place.

i. Overseeing the implementation and operationalization of both the strategic policy and strategic plan.

6.3. Composition Of BOT:

There is no specific instruction to ensure that one gender is more dominant than the other. Common sense requires that when selecting BOT members, one tries as much as possible to ensure gender balancing.

When picking individuals to be invited to your board, please note the following:

1. The registration requirements for the organization do not specify that your board member has to be a rich man, a wealthy woman, a powerful man or woman, a popular actor, a famous imam, or the wife of a known politician.

2. The registration requirements for the organization do not ask you for the best man on the street, the oldest woman in the neighborhood, or the coolest guy around.

3. What the registration requirement for all organizations states is that it is for men and women of integrity, of notable character, who have not been convicted of any crimes and are of good standing in the communities, and such a person can be an ordinary man or woman with impeccable character.

4. What the law requires is that since the personal qualities of board members are critical to the board's and organization's success, the following qualities must be prioritized;

(a) Moral and professional integrity, **(b)** Not a known criminal or one with criminal records **(c)** Relevant professional competence, **(d)** Broad insights, **(e)** Dedication and **(f)** Potentials

Without doubt, when selecting a viable member, one wants the best individual who has time to share with the organization and has the interests of the organization at heart. The following are some of the qualities of a good BOT member brings on the table:

1. Passion: deep interest in the mission of your

organization.

2. Vision and leadership— the ability to see the big picture and the courage to set direction to achieve the organization's mission

3. Stewardship: the integrity to serve the interests and pursue the goals of your organization, as well as the interests of the public and your organization's intended beneficiaries.

4. Experienced or knowledgeable in the areas of the organization's target groups and style of operations, with some modicum of organizational and managerial capacity.

5. Diligence: dedication and commitment to fulfilling the organization's goals and objectives

6. Collegiality: possessing a sincere and respectful attitude toward colleagues and their views.

7. Discretion: ability to maintain the confidentiality of board discussions and speaks with one voice when representing the organization in the

community.

It might also be useful to include, as part of the induction references for a newly constituted board, that, to be an effective board member, it is hoped that each member will come to the table;

(1) Bringing their cumulated personal experiences, interests, and expertise to the non-profit organization, but bearing in mind that their primary obligation of stewardship is to the organization as a whole. **(2)** Come to meetings on time; **(3)** Be attentive and well prepared at all meetings. **(4)** Respect disagreement without personalizing the debates and avoid crisis in the face of dissent. **(6)** Ask questions rather than accepting the status quo. **(7)** Welcoming information and advice, but reserving the right to make decisions based on your own best judgment. **(8)** Support the board's decisions as well as the professional staff that you have appointed to serve the organization.

***

It is not unusual but actually practical for the founder(s) of the organisation to be a member of the Board. In most cases, members of the Board are happy to vote for the proprietor as Chairman/Chairwoman to preside over the Board. However, what is usual and likely to cause bias against the organisation and its leadership is when the Board is jam-packed with family members, making the organisation erroneously appear as a family business. One or two family member is sufficient—if at all necessary.

7. Branding and Communication

An organization that intends to stand out in the minds of its target groups and donors must strategically reconsider its brand positioning, if it already has one, or create one that makes it stand out if it has none. Brand positioning, if done effectively, allows the organization to stay top-of-mind with its targets and partners.

It's useful and strategic for organizations to have an official communication strategy. In some cases, some organizations just overlook these aspects of standardizing their organizations and their operations, partly because they feel it is unimportant. But it is very important because it is an identity issue. Every staff must be aware of that in the organization; communication (both internal and external) is to be taken as seriously as possible. For example, the organization's policy must include a clearly marked writing tool that is comprehensively understood by staff and made to be used while making official communications. Such tools include

1. Font type,

2. Font style, and

3. Font size

For its communication with an external organization or people, there must be an agreed-upon and acceptable style. It means that if any staff member writes with any other font aside from that provided in the policy guide, it may create identity confusion in the minds of partners. For consistency, partners must know an organization with a consistent, constant, and unique style.

For Example: HELWEI adopts "Tahoma Font" as its font style, size 12, and style normal as its communication identity on every electronically generated communication.

Color is also an integral part of identity in communication. The color selected must not only be color for its own sake but must also speak to the overall goal, objective, and intention of the organization. Any disconnection between the goals, objectives, and colors indicates a confusion of intention, a confusion of strategy, and a structural disconnect in the entire process.

> ***Example:*** *HELWEI will use green and lemon. The color green in the HELWEI communication identity stands for fertility of the soil, the greens of vegetation, and the association of fresh green with healthy plantations. The color green also helps HELWEI to communicate that its goal is productivity, closeness to nature, health, usefulness, and a life-saving agriculture engagement project.*

What this means is that every poster, every sign board, and every piece of information material that is used to represent the organization must contain all these characteristics. The name of the organization must be in the approved font type. The background color of their banners and billboards should be in approved colors, with approved font types. Consequently, their graphic designers and external consultants should be reminded of these communication styles.

A proper organization's branding is part of successful marketing and standards.

8. Monitoring And Evaluation

Monitoring and Evaluation is a technique that development organizations use to track changes and the impact of their work. In recent times, monitoring and evaluation have become an implementable mechanism and relevant tool that donors depend on to ensure that the resources they provided for their partner organizations are adequately and judiciously utilized on the project for which they were applied. Some serious donors insist on both internal and external evaluations of the use of their grant.

8.1. Monitoring:

From the word "monitoring, this means ensuring that a program is going according to plan. Monitoring is the systematic process of collecting, analyzing, and using information to track a program's progress toward reaching its objectives and to guide management's decisions in proceeding with or stopping such a process. Monitoring usually focuses on processes, such as when and where activities are occurring, who is delivering them, how the target groups are appreciating the processes, and the number of people or entities the program is reaching.

8.2. Evaluation:

An evaluation is an appraisal of a project to see if it achieved its set goals. Evaluation is also a mechanism to assess if the strategies used in executing the project worked, if the policies were the right ones, if the environment was supportive of the program, if the beneficiaries were happier for it, and if the general performance was as hoped. It also includes appraising the competences of the organization that executed the project, its human and financial resource availability for the project, and placing all these variables against what was achieved—the failure or success of the projects under evaluation.

The goal of M&E is to collect data for analysis to appraise and ascertain the impact of a project under evaluation with a view to determining and, if possible, improving the impact, and to also obtain lessons learned for the sake of future project input, output, outcome, and impact.

Evaluation refers to the analysis of the end results of a project against the initial projection (baseline) of the project.

What this means, for example, is that if a project proposes to reduce infant mortality rates by certain periods, the evaluation of the project would ask and seek answers to the following questions:

1. *What was the **baseline** study report before the commencement of the project? This will provide the bases for evaluating "progress" made. Such status as the number of child deaths in the previous years and what was previously done to curb the*

abnormality. Whatever we capture against our intervention, will be reviewed as achievement over the baseline

2. *Did infant mortality reduce as a result of the intervention?*

3. *Is there an impact as a result of the project we did?*

4. *Are there noticeable impacts?*

5. *What did the project do right?*

6. *What did the project do wrong?*

7. *How were the roles of the organization, its leadership, its staff, and its consultant in ensuring project impacts?*

8. *What are the lessons learned?*

Some donors recommend mid-term and end-term evaluations of projects. Mid-term evaluation of the project is done mid-way prior to completion of the project. The midterm evaluation can influence a re-direction of the program or restructuring of the operation for a more effective outcome. The other importance of a mid-term evaluation is that if the project is not going according to plan, it can be easily terminated.

The end-term evaluation is the evaluation at the completion of the project.

8.3. Lesson learned:

This is an evaluation technique where the evaluator interrogates the processes of engagement. For example, to determine if a project went well, questions like these will come up.

1. *Was the success a result of the expertise of the organization; the techniques employed, and the collaborations of both partners and target groups?*

2. *How will you rate the professionalism of the program handlers?*

3. *Was the success recorded as a result of target group's eagerness to receive impact?*

4. *How was the impact of the project's timing?*

Lessons learned also include

1. *What was responsible for the failure?*

2. *Who was responsible for the failure?*

3. *How did we get failure? Was it a result of poor program planning, or was it inappropriate for the target group?*

4. *Was it the risk and assumptions that affected program implementation, and what were the mitigation plans?*

Lesson learned is technique of evaluation, which helps the organization replicate success and/or to help the organization avoid future failures. "Lessons learned" is an integral evaluation tool that helps the organization acquire more expertise. It is an assessment where an organization tells itself the truth about:

1. *Its actual level of impact*

2. *Its ability to deliver on its set goals*

3. *The status and competences of its staff and leadership*

4. *The relevance of the organization in its target communities and*

5. *The appropriateness of its thematic relevance*

Note 4: *Lessons learned are usually not for the donor but for the organization to use to correct itself, adjust its operation (style and delivery), appraise effectiveness (on the fields and preparedness for engagements), give itself thumbs up where projects are well implemented, congratulate staff, appreciate effort, commend dedications, applaud volunteers, and reward consistency.*

9. Logical Framework

Monitoring and evaluation, as earlier explained, starts with a detailed understanding of the various processes of every project to be implemented. There are standard processes that make evaluations easier for everyone (*both internal and external evaluators*) to conduct and allow the organisation itself to track changes and achievements without requiring an external person to confirm what it already knows. These standard processes are laid out in a clear and understandable **logical framework** where the laid sequences *lead to expected output and outcome,* including *what is verifiable as impact or achievement claims*. What is to be evaluated then are the project claims—if they actually happened—and if they confirm each objectively verifiable indicator and demonstrate to an independent evaluator, each concrete achievements.

The diagram below is a suggested LogFrame model. It highlights key words that are essential when developing a logframe, i.e.,

1. Overall Objective,

2. Specific Objective

3. Input,

4. Output

5. Indicator

6. Objectively Verifiable Indicator (OVI)

7. Key Performance Indicator (KPI)

8. Outcome

9. Assumption

Homework on Coaching and Feedback

HELWEI was provided the opportunity to gain practical experiences completing a LogFrame. *The assignment was to implement a grant regime for beneficiaries in the Egbeda Areas of their primary target.* The homework was:

Draft Program Activities For a "Potential Grant"

1. Identification of the target groups

2. Identification of the needs of target groups

3. Grant engagement modalities are mapped out.

4. Training and sensitization on skill acquisition for participants

5. Placement of beneficiaries in firms or vocational centers to learn on the job

6. Training on team building and networking, Regular or scheduled meetings of the association; choosing the name of the organization; registration with authorities

7. Financial management training, interaction with financial institutions, Opening bank accounts for disbursements

8. Microcredit scheme for the selected beneficiaries

9. Mid-Term evaluation

10. Payback schedules

11. Evaluation of the project

The response is in the table below. The answers are contained in the following colors:

Section Four: Creating Sustainability: Strategy and Implementation Tips

10. Resource Mobilization and Fundraising

There are many people, both individuals and groups of friends, who would like to make impacts in societies, who would like to touch lives, effect changes in their communities, or provide education or political enlightenment for their constituents. The only thing standing in the way of engaging in this charitable venture is access to funds and other resources to use for it. So let us explore how to access funds.

Fundraising is the heartbeat of civil society organizations and the oil that propels all the activities and intentions of that organization or its efforts to help others. Without funds, there are only a few things to do and hardly much to achieve in terms of impact. Therefore, the roles that funds play are greatly immeasurable. This chapter then focuses on the different processes involved in fundraising for charity organizations.

Setting up an NGO involves costs, which must be paid one way or another. The hard costs of opening offices and maintaining them; the hard costs of recruiting competent staff, even when some of the staff are volunteers (*there are costs involved in providing stipends or other support for the volunteers to be able to effectively perform their assigned tasks*); these are some of the costs involved in setting up an organization of this nature; there are still costs involved in the actual program formulations and implementations. Knowing well that an NGO is not a profitable organization, the practical question becomes how these costs are to be estimated and funded.

Generally, I believe that efforts aimed at supporting communities, the state, or target groups are not the burden of one person, irrespective of the financial buoyancy of such a person. It should involve shared project commitments and joint efforts. Shared with the communities and beneficiaries. When the project is the result of joint efforts and shared commitments, it is mostly likely to be more enduring, and its sustainability is halfway achieved. The argument for seeking strong alliances or shared commitments is practical because the joint owners will ensure the organization remains alive. Shared ownership or joint commitment does not only depersonalize the project; it also gives room for the growth of the association and gives opportunity for previous beneficiaries to give back to the community when they can because, after all, it is a project for all, and *all* (or, at least, by some estimations, some of the beneficiaries) should be part of its funding. Our sages say, "*Àgbájo owó la fí n sò'yà, owó kan ò gbé'rù d'órí*", that it is with collective efforts (not individual efforts) that difficult tasks are performed with minimal stress. Fundraising is easy, but that exercise hinges on two conditions that cannot be taken with a cavalier attitude:

1. The organization must be fully registered (preferably with CAC, which is the ultimate NGO registration platform in the case of a Nigeria-based NGO).

2. The organization must have at least, one bank account that is completely in its name with clear mandates for multiple signatories. The bank accounts can not be by proxy. The organization must have been fully registered with the governments and their agencies to have a bank account.

11. Strategies For Resource Mobilization

Funding is generally considered as the wheel of progress. Nothing can be achieved without the role that funds play. The following is a list of suggested fundraising strategies that any NGO can use to raise funds for its operations or capacity building. They are;

1. Private fundraising
2. Donations and charity
3. Donor agencies (local or foreign agencies)
4. Cost share
5. Tokenism
6. Private celebration events into fundraising
7. Corporate Social Responsibilities (CSR)
8. Volunteerism

9. Non-finance-based fundraising

10. Bazar Sales

11.1. Private Fundraising:

In a frank and honest view, the initial costs of creating the organization (however modest) need to be covered by the founder of the organization. Unless the project is community-initiated or a partnership between like-minded individuals, the initial operational cost is to be borne by the founder. In today's reality, hardly any external donor partner will commit funds to starting an organization that is not already in operation, or, as a commonly used phrase goes, "on the ground" with demonstrable achievements and competencies. It is technically prudent to ensure that the operational costs are covered and activities are already initiated before inviting others to come in and give funds. Nonetheless, where the founder of the organization is buoyant enough, it is also okay to continue to fund the organization, its programs, and its projects and to take pride in the impact recorded. However, it is advisable that every resource to be shared for both operational and programmatic costs be given to the organization through its official bank account and dispensed according to its laid-down financial processes. This is because when auditors come (and the organization will be audited), auditors can only audit money that has been properly processed and not dotted out in cash.

11.2. Donation and Charity:

Donations are also another way of generating resources for managing NGOs to create impact. Donations can come from friends, partners, cooperating organizations, religious bodies, and even some anonymous donors.

11.3. Donor Agencies:

Seeking funds from donor agencies is perhaps the most symbolic way of raising funds. This is because these are organizations set up to support local organizations where they have offices. Seeking partnership or collaboration with donor agencies does not require romanticizing the donors to get favors from them (like one will do to woo private donors), but in this case, one will be dealing with a formal and principled institution with clearly laid out processes for supporting NGOs. To seek foreign donors, the organization must have done its homework, which includes proper articulations of its core thematic focus and areas of activities. There can be no uncertainties about such an organization's work, its relevance, its leadership, or its antecedents. In most cases, foreign donors advertise the availability of their funds along with the process of accessing the funds. Another way of partnering with donors is through direct relationships, where foreign donors approach NGOs for unpublished funding. Where the foreign donors advertise the availability of their fund in an "open call" or "call for proposals (CfP), there are guidelines and conditions attached to the call that must be adhered to in order to win the grants. Although some established NGOs fear approaching donor agencies, they provide the partnership for NGO initiatives. To apply for donor funds, it is required to understand the following principles:

1. Seek out the guidelines for the CfP, read the guidelines thoroughly, and understand them. Some of them, i.e., the EU, even have platforms

for seeking clarifications to their guidelines. It is essential to have a comprehensive understanding of the guidelines. Where you are working in a team, mandate every member to read the manual and discuss the content so that everyone on the team is on the same page throughout. This point is very key and essential to winning a bid or CfP.

2. Follow the guidelines provided for the grant. Ensure that you read, understand, and accept what the guidelines recommend for you to do. Kindly refrain from the idea of interpreting the guidelines as "this is what they mean," because what they mean is what they wrote down, and you must follow without anticipating what you think they might or ought to mean.

3. Ensure that the project you want to implement is clear, well-articulated, and very straightforward. It does not have to have Shakespearean or Oxford-level English; its simplicity is your best bet of gaining attention or winning. Ensure that there are very few ambiguities, if any.

4. Use the logical framework matrix like the one above. Once you have constructed a meaningful LogFrame, the rest is simple because the intended project that you want to submit would have already made sense to you before you tried to persuade others to see the sense in it. It is easier to make sense to others outside your office once the processes—meaning, the goals, the objectives, the ways of tracking achievements, and the type of impact you want to achieve—are first made logical to yourself.

5. Be modest in your fund request: it is critical to ensure you do not apply for funds that are way beyond the capacity of the organization. An example is this: why will an organization that has never managed a million naira put up an application for ten million naira? If this amount is minimal, then work in collaboration or partnership with another close NGO to put up a joint proposal, sharing projects, expanding targets to reach, and ensuring that all partners have clearly defined roles and functions.

6. Use of experienced proposal writers: proposal writing is a technical competence. Not everyone who speaks English can put up a development proposal because it is not about the language's competence but about projects and impact; it is about program development, their output, and most significantly, their projected logical outcome. Do not be afraid to ask experts for assistance or to consult other NGO staff who are more competent at writing proposals for large donor organizations to check out what you put together, but be careful who you ask to ensure that a blind man is not leading another blind. Abèrè ònà kìí sìnà: s/he who asks others for direction of where he is going does not miss the way. Keep practicing and doing things yourself to improve your own ability and confidence. Competencies are obtained through practice, so keep practicing after your last session.

11.4. Cost Share:

Cost share originated as a USAID coined language. What they expect under a cost-sharing funding regime is that the organization to be funded must also have some cost responsibilities to undertake during the implementation of the program they provided funds for. In a broader sense, cost-share is a way of raising funds. There are many ways of using cost-share as a fundraising technique. For example, if an organization intends to implement a project somewhere for the benefit of the intended beneficiaries, it could open up the possibility of sharing the costs of the implementation with stakeholders in those communities. Stakeholders, such as the direct beneficiaries, the recipient community, or the implementors of the project. For example, the community can provide venues, chairs, fresh water, and other useful implements that make the processes flow with the minimum of hitches, including supplementing refreshments, while the NGO only comes in with its technical expertise and staff to conduct the project. It is easier to bear the burden of costs when they are shared. Two additional things to note about "cost share"

1. Be prepared to present cost-sharing calculations when approaching an international donor for collaboration or support. In whatever case, donors will always appreciate cost-share calculations when making grant applications. Cost-share is not only cash but can also be in kind. i.e., office rents, staff salaries, logistic calculations, and other costs that the donor grants will not cover but will be used in the project implementation can be inserted in the cost-share calculation. You will not present the entire costs of your office rents and other costs as cost-share, but an agreed-upon percentage of these costs. It is assumed that the office is not for this project alone but for others as well. Percentage of the costs is descent and expected.

2. Always build a cost-share approach into your programming; allow the beneficiaries to also share certain costs, no matter how small. The period when NGOs pay delegates to conferences and

training are fast becoming impracticable, there is little resources to go around, so the in-thing is to cost-share. Allow the beneficiary's costs to be shared in the collaborative language like "We will do so, so, and so much for you; what will you do for yourself?"

11.5. Tokenism:

This is similar to the cost-share calculation. Tokenism is a funding strategy of fundraising by pushing the costs of implementation of programs to those who benefit directly from the project impact. It is to require from the beneficiaries a token, or a predetermined fraction, of the cost of participation in the program activities so as to share the burden of the costs involved. This mark of tokenism also extends to facility providers, where the organization requests the providers for discounts and waivers in their facility rates and charges. There are also some aspects of donor funds that are excluded from taxes and VAT. When these are taken out, the cost of program implementation is grossly bearable.

11.6. Turning private celebration events into fundraising:

Another hardly explored strategy of fundraising is to transform private events into public fundraising events for the NGO. Examples are when a benefactor chooses to turn his or her birthday celebration, wedding anniversary, or special thanksgiving event into a fundraising occasion, thereby appealing to friends, associates, and admirers to identify a good project(s) and donate towards such a project. An easier way of doing this is to ask friends to convert presents and gifts into cash and donate it to an NGO. Another way is to say, "No party, no celebration; the resources earmarked for the party and celebration should be donated to a good cause!

11.7. Corporate Social Responsibilities- CSR:

There is a law encouraging, or in some cases, compelling, corporate organizations to support humanitarian and not-for-profit activities that NGOs represent through their projects. The challenge is to identify friendly corporate institutions and to lobby them to accept your NGOs as one of the beneficiaries of their CSR. In another sense, the onus is on the NGO to convince corporate organizations to invest in communities where they operate through their expanded CSR programs with your NGO. It is to be noted that CSR is not a moral or humanitarian gift from the corporate institutions; whatever they give through CSR is deductible from tax, making them less liable in their mega profits.

11.8. Volunteerism:

This is when gifted and talented individuals choose to make contributions to the work of the organization by donating their time, experience, and availability to help implement projects. Volunteers have talents and skills to provide on the basis of helping to support charitable acts. Volunteers are often not paid, and, in some cases, aside from donating their skills and talents, they make other financial donations towards implementation. The NGO must position itself to attract high-quality volunteers.

11.9. Non-Finance based fundraising:

The purpose of fundraising is to implement projects. There are other, hardly explored project implementations that are based on material donations. A project does not necessarily depend solely on finances. Public enlightenment can be conducted in open spaces, market spaces, churches, schools, event centers, mosques, town halls, and so on. The strategy is to identify partners who are willing to share these non-finance-based supports towards the implementation of activities aimed at helping the less privileged.

11.10. Bazaar Sales:

The church or religious organizations have mastered this act; they collect disposable items from congregations and sell them to interested people as charity items and then use the money gained for other purposes. Organizing similar social enterprises, soliciting donations of materials to sell, and participating in bazaar enterprises clearly labeled non-profit or charity, where all revenue generated from products sold and/or services provided is channelled towards conducting the organization's mission(s), which include donations, grants, sponsorships, and so on.

The top takeaway here is to create an organization that is self-sustaining and independent of external donors. But the caveat is that if you can develop an organization that can self-sustain without corporate sponsorship or grants, you will inadvertently be attracted to corporate sponsorship and grants from those who want to share in your successes and who think you must be credible enough to have achieved so much.

Chapter Twelve

12. Sustainability

Sustainability: The Strategy of Continued Impact

The age-old aphorism that "*what is worth doing at all is worth doing well*" is the background of the discussions on this sustainably part. Right from the inception of any CSO, the initiators must have the short and long-term goals and be prepared for whatever it takes to go the long haul. keeping in mind that it is not an organization set up just to access funds and then close shop, but one that stays with its target group for as long as possible because development is not one time project or specific time bound. If this is the case, then the strategies and plans must always look at the distant future and not the immediate future of their program and existence.

The following are sustainability strategy suggestions that organizations can adopt.

1. **Self-Promotion**

Even though they are not for profit, NGOs modestly do little to engage in promoting what they do so others know that they exist and are out there. It is out of being modest—focusing on the work done and its impact rather than popularizing itself. However, NGOs have to use aggressive relationship management and social media to remain relevant and grow exponentially like normal corporate organizations. Organizations have to invest in promoting what they do. They have to develop a concrete strategy for doing this. No one but the organization will sell itself.

2. **Partnerships**

Developing partnerships and sponsorship from large organizations, as well as partnerships with other non-governmental organizations, is a good strategy for ensuring the sustainability of the organization. One of such partnership exists with the UNDP's promotion of Sustainable Development Goals. The intention is to ensure that whatever development that is happening must be capable of being sustained and continuous even beyond a funding regime. Such SDG as,

Planting the trees for the future

planting trees, protecting the environment, ensuring that "water flows in its natural path". There are several organisations ready to partner on these issues of SDGs.

3. **Pay-It-Forward**

Building and facilitating community engagement in such a way that an active community of beneficiaries would become advocates and grassroots fundraisers for the organization. In this way, I think of the concept of "paying it forward," which involves letting beneficiaries also show charity to others. *Pay it forward is an expression for describing the beneficiary of a good deed repaying the kindness to others instead of to the original benefactor.*

- "Social Enterprise Infusion" Create a product or service that would generate revenue for your nonprofit or charity while adding value to its users.

- "Social Media Positioning": Use your social media

handles for maximum traffic generation and convert that traffic into a support base. Social media handlers must be fully engaged in their interactions, responsive, and see the connection between friendly interactions and the reputation of the NGO

Mechanism for Seeking Partnerships and Collaborators:

1. The first question to be raised is, What is the organisation's fundraising plan? Is there any on the ground for reference, reviews, and institutionalisation?

2. The second question is, Does the organisation have any experts volunteering with it in the areas of resource mobilisation?

3. Does the organisation plan to attend other events, and how often does it intend to allow its staff to participate in other organised projects and activities? Aside from learning from others, peer networking is key to increasing relevance. At these organised events, collaborations are strengthened, partnerships are reinforced, and others get to know that your organisation exists and is available for joint efforts.

4. There are direct and indirect calls for proposals.

This means that there are some organisations that might need to be approached directly to inquire about partnerships, while others only require responses to their published CfP.

It is important to consider each of these approaches carefully and be strategic in your choices. In the case that the NGO intends to be donor-dependent, then, a fairly comprehensive list of international aid or "donor agencies" is available on Wikipedia, along with links to their websites. It might be a good idea to glance over this list and take some time to read over the many organisations on this list and seek to understand their various areas of support. Before approaching them for partnerships and support, it is important to first understand them, their support needs, and their mode of operation. The list can be found here: https://en.wikipedia.org/wiki/List_of_development_aid_agencies

There is also a global "*Fund for NGOs*" that lives up to its name and provides a good number of advertised grants for NGOs to apply for and shortlist. It can be found here: https://www.fundsforngos.org.

Books and Articles consulted

Books read and Articles consulted during the preparation for this book

1. The EU-British Council ACT Program in Nigeria: conceptnote and ToR

2. EU-ACP Concept Notes and Documents

3. Civil society: An essential ingredient of development, George Ingram, Monday, April 6, 2020

4. "The Function and Impact of Civil Societies and Civil Society Organizations," Gabby Turner, Virginia's Blue Ridge. Georgia's Coastal Plain, 2016

5. Rachel Cooper, "What is Civil Society, its Role and

Value in 2018?" January 2019

6. The Man of The People, Chinua Achebe, 1966

7. Cover   Pictures:
   https://www.istockphoto.com/search/2/image?p
   hrase=ngo+africa

8. Cover   Pictures:
   https://www.opindia.com/2017/04/center-and-su
   preme-court-tighten-the-screws-to-make-ngos-m
   ore-accountable-for-their-actions/

1. The Cotonou Agreement is a treaty between the European Union and the African, Caribbean, and Pacific Group of States ("ACP countries"). It was signed in June 2000 in Cotonou, Benin's largest city, by 78 ACP countries (Cuba did not sign) and the then fifteen Member States of the European Union.

2. EU-ACP Agreement, June 2000

3. https://www.cac.gov.ng/incorporated-trustees/?__cf_chl_jschl_tk__=f4b6b6491e091eecfcb8310a78244c84f567cfb0-1614090715-0-ASQ-pqh5rY4a0WHfxXPvUcxcdxGB25uUxkbdrphtQZlYhkZG1QVlOtS6xyn4PbOoMYe8BcWiIfEEdsQ24Em8RaD8VHiLw75x3XV0hLa7qiNO368El_78VRvGG2yDDZq4MUzzKcQCB37I9m0ld5d_kls8lwvhnaW4FrO0iIlPgIPtyk41Z452Mli0_xlnt6-pigLflB6Aur324AvV8JEt1Znuh7ccqvmp1iaCgv0mvEggp_vJ8dx10XKO6veDv8sPWkC2P-9rP9arfkMg3DafjoBTF_D_-Tu0DjFgvbrsXJyY5_biaMt-MlLFxaWrhaoaduy2Y_EeZLqewfCcq_Dyv0U

4. https://concordeurope.org/cross-cutting-priorities/civil-society-power/#:~:text=Civil%20society%20organisations%20amplify%20the,to%20account%20for%20their%20commitments.

About Author

'Délé A. Sónúbi has engaged in creative writing since his youth. He began this hobby when he started writing, directing, and acting in staged dramas right from primary school and continued through the various universities and academic institutions that he attended. The experiences obtained through these hobbies helped in shaping his fictional characters, formulating dialogues, composing folklore songs and poetry, as well as his non-creative writings such as speeches and essays. *Délé* has advanced degrees in philosophy, culture, peace, and development studies from universities in Nigeria, Spain, Austria, and Denmark. He continues to work for peace and social cohesion. He believes in multi-ethnic and transcultural diversity and engages in research that amplifies African philosophies and indigenous initiatives. He seeks knowledge at the expense of knowledge and for the sake of knowledge.

Other Books By Same Author

1. The Grandfather's Mandate

2. The Ultimate Success that Overcame Failures

3. When Faith Defiled Reasons: The Testimony Of A Phantom Negotiation With God

4. The Solitude of Roving Feet: Empathy In Chants

5. The Lord's Prayers (Playlet)

6. The Miracle That Keeps You in Awe (Playlet)

7. The Armed Robbers 1 & 2: And Other Stories

8. Learning How To Help Others: A Guide For Starting & Sustaining An NGO

9. Ariya Ti De: The Biography of Àhújà-Bello Omo Ebedí Moko, Ìséyìn